"Space, the fina..."

STAR TREK

NCC-1701

U.S.S. ENTERPRISE

"I'VE ALREADY GOT A FEMALE TO WORRY ABOUT."
— KIRK

STAR TREK

STAR DATE: _____

"...to boldly go where no man has gone before."

TM ® & © 2006 Paramount Pictures. All rights reserved.

STAR TREK

NCC-1701

U.S.S. ENTERPRISE

"CRAZY WAY TO TRAVEL ... SPREADING A MAN'S MOLECULES ALL OVER THE UNIVERSE." —McCOY

STAR TREK

STAR DATE: _____

"...to explore strange new worlds..."

TM ® & © 2006 Paramount Pictures. All rights reserved.

STAR TREK

NCC-1701

U.S.S. ENTERPRISE

"LIVE LONG AND PROSPER." —SPOCK

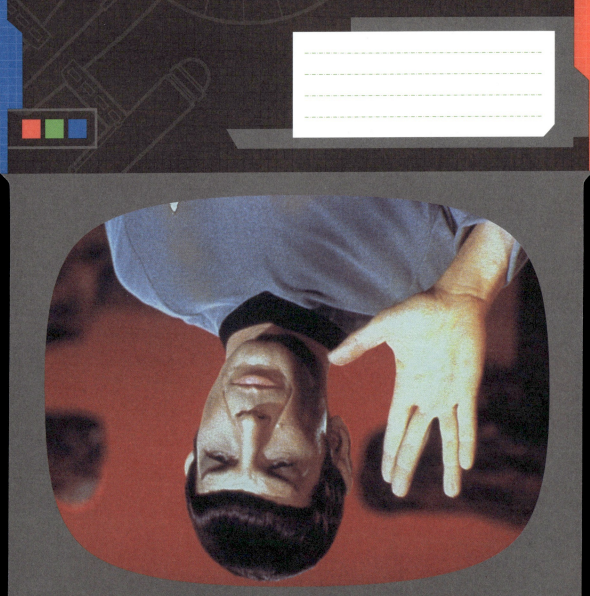

STAR TREK

STAR DATE: _____

"These are the voyages of the Starship Enterprise."

STAR TREK

"WARP SPEED AHEAD." —KIRK

NCC-1701

U.S.S. ENTERPRISE

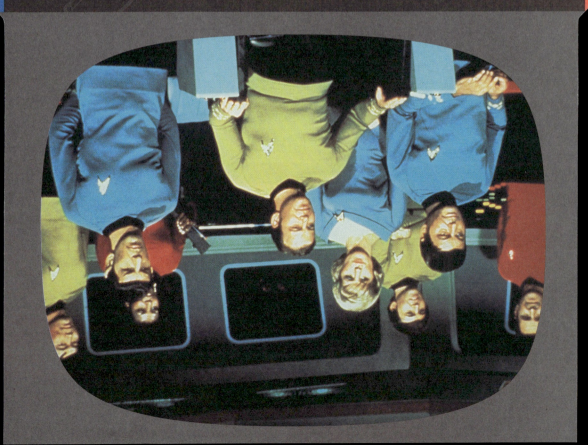

STAR TREK

STAR DATE: _____

"...to seek out new life and new civilizations..."

U.S.S. ENTERPRISE NCC-1701

STAR TREK™

NCC-1701

U.S.S. ENTERPRISE

"IT'S A HUMAN CHARACTERISTIC TO LOVE LITTLE ANIMALS, ESPECIALLY IF THEY'RE ATTRACTIVE IN SOME WAY." —KIRK

STAR TREK

STAR DATE: _____

"Space, the final frontier."

TM ® & © 2006 Paramount Pictures. All rights reserved.

STAR TREK

NCC-1701

U.S.S. ENTERPRISE

"I'VE ALREADY GOT A FEMALE TO WORRY ABOUT." – KIRK

STAR DATE: _____

STAR TREK

"...to boldly go where no man has gone before."

TM ® & © 2006 Paramount Pictures. All rights reserved.

STAR TREK™

"CRAZY WAY TO TRAVEL... SPREADING A MAN'S MOLECULES ALL OVER THE UNIVERSE." — McCOY

NCC-1701

U.S.S. ENTERPRISE

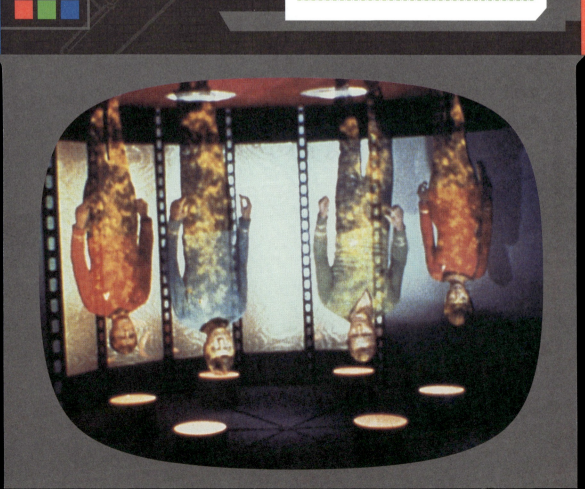

STAR DATE: _____

STAR TREK

"...to explore strange new worlds..."

STAR TREK

NCC-1701

U.S.S. ENTERPRISE

"LIVE LONG AND PROSPER," —SPOCK

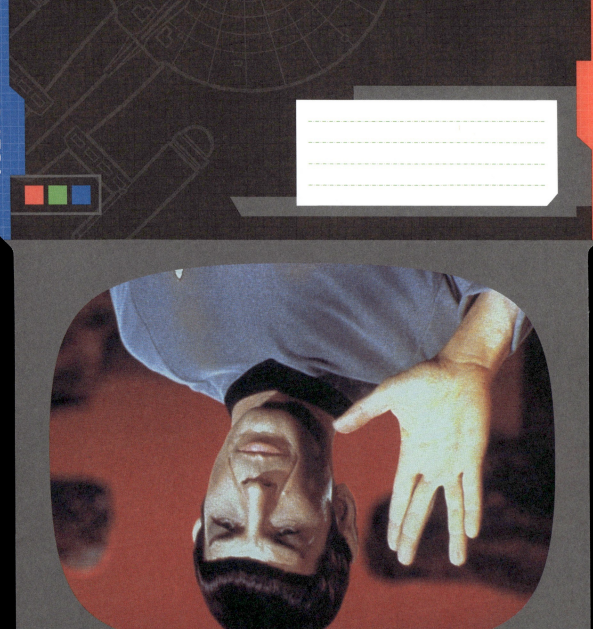

STAR TREK

STAR DATE: _____

"These are the voyages of the Starship Enterprise."

TM ® & © 2006 Paramount Pictures. All rights reserved.

STAR TREK™

"WARP SPEED AHEAD." —KIRK

U.S.S. ENTERPRISE

NCC-1701

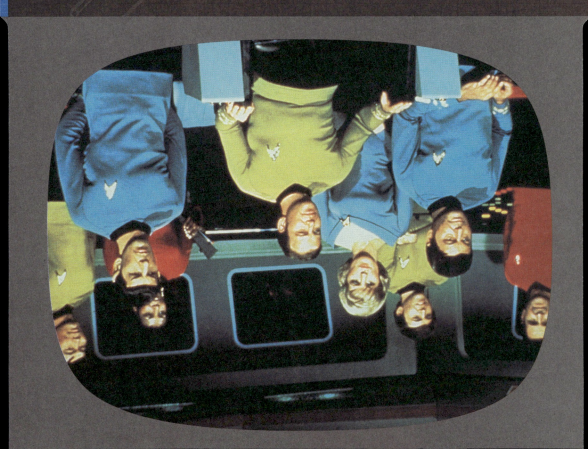

STAR TREK

"...to seek out new life and new civilizations..."

STAR DATE: _____

U.S.S. ENTERPRISE NCC-1701

TM ® & © 2006 Paramount Pictures. All rights reserved.

"IT'S A HUMAN CHARACTERISTIC TO LOVE LITTLE ANIMALS, ESPECIALLY IF THEY'RE ATTRACTIVE IN SOME WAY." - KIRK

STAR TREK

NCC-1701

U.S.S. ENTERPRISE

STAR TREK

"Space, the final frontier."

STAR DATE: _____

STAR TREK

NCC-1701

U.S.S. ENTERPRISE

"I'VE ALREADY GOT A FEMALE TO WORRY ABOUT. HER NAME IS ENTERPRISE." – KIRK

STAR TREK

STAR DATE: _____

"...to boldly go where no man has gone before."

STAR TREK

"CRAZY WAY TO TRAVEL... SPREADING A MAN'S MOLECULES ALL OVER THE UNIVERSE." – McCOY

NCC-1701

U.S.S. ENTERPRISE

STAR TREK

STAR DATE: _____

"...to explore strange new worlds..."

TM ® & © 2006 Paramount Pictures. All rights reserved.

STAR TREK

"LIVE LONG AND PROSPER." —SPOCK

NCC-1701

U.S.S. ENTERPRISE

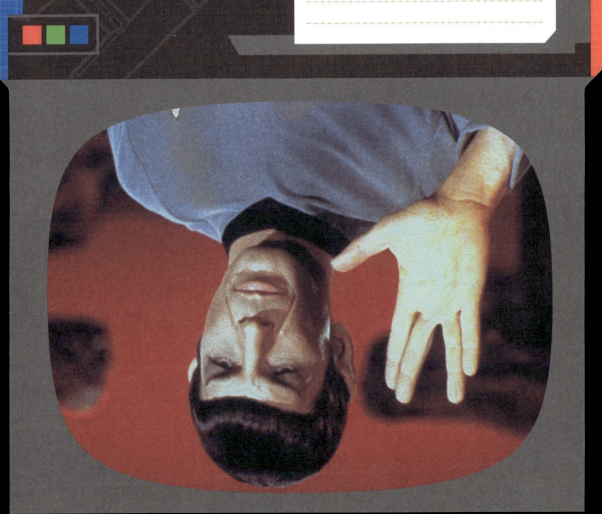

STAR DATE: _____

STAR TREK

"These are the voyages of the Starship Enterprise."

TM ® & © 2006 Paramount Pictures. All rights reserved.

STAR TREK

"WARP SPEED AHEAD." —KIRK

U.S.S. ENTERPRISE

NCC-1701

STAR TREK

"...to seek out new life and new civilizations..."

STAR DATE: _____

U.S.S. ENTERPRISE NCC-1701

TM ® & © 2006 Paramount Pictures. All rights reserved.

STAR TREK™

"IT'S A HUMAN CHARACTERISTIC TO LOVE LITTLE ANIMALS."

NCC-1701

U.S.S. ENTERPRISE

STAR TREK

"Space, the final frontier."

STAR DATE: _____

"I'VE ALREADY GOT A FEMALE TO WORRY ABOUT. HER NAME IS ENTERPRISE." –KIRK

STAR TREK

NCC-1701

U.S.S. ENTERPRISE

STAR DATE: _____

STAR TREK

"...to boldly go where no man has gone before."

TM ® & © 2006 Paramount Pictures. All rights reserved.

STAR TREK

NCC-1701

U.S.S. ENTERPRISE

"CRAZY WAY TO TRAVEL... SPREADING A MAN'S

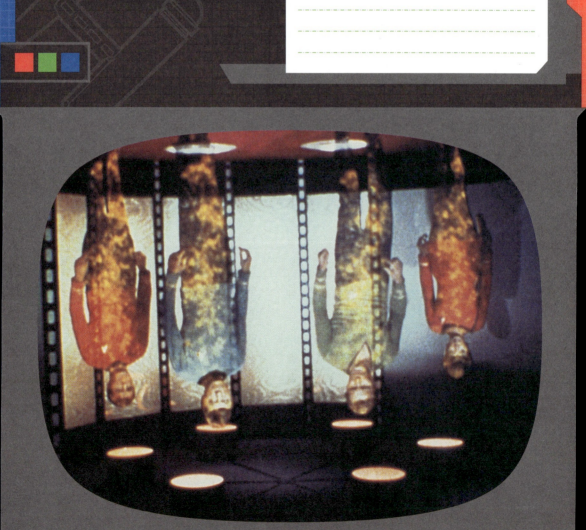

STAR TREK

STAR DATE: _____

"...to explore strange new worlds..."

STAR TREK

"LIVE LONG AND PROSPER." —SPOCK

U.S.S. ENTERPRISE

NCC-1701

STAR TREK

STAR DATE: _____

"These are the voyages of the Starship Enterprise."

TM ® & © 2006 Paramount Pictures. All rights reserved.

STAR TREK™

"WARP SPEED AHEAD." —KIRK

NCC-1701

U.S.S. ENTERPRISE

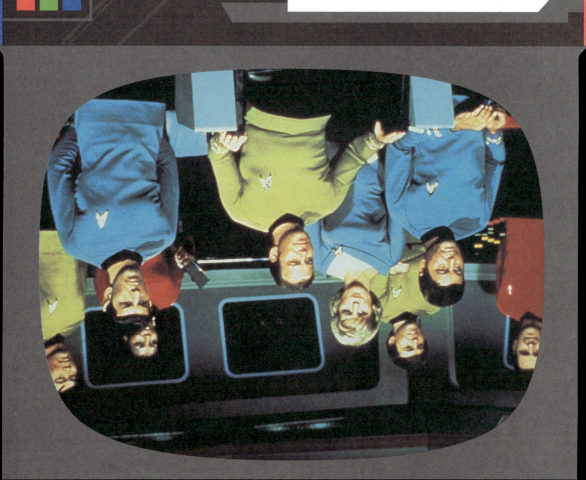

STAR TREK

STAR DATE: _____

"...to seek out new life and new civilizations..."

U.S.S. ENTERPRISE
NCC-1701

TM ® & © 2006 Paramount Pictures. All rights reserved.

"IT'S A HUMAN CHARACTERISTIC TO LOVE LITTLE ANIMALS, ESPECIALLY IF THEY'RE ATTRACTIVE IN SOME WAY." –KIRK

STAR TREK

U.S.S. ENTERPRISE

NCC-1701

STAR TREK

"Space, the final frontier."

STAR DATE: _____

STAR TREK

NCC-1701

U.S.S. ENTERPRISE

"I'VE ALREADY GOT A FEMALE TO WORRY ABOUT. HER NAME'S THE ENTERPRISE."

STAR TREK

STAR DATE: _____

"...to boldly go where no man has gone before."

STAR TREK

"CRAZY WAY TO TRAVEL... SPREADING A MAN'S MOLECULES ALL OVER THE UNIVERSE."

NCC-1701

U.S.S. ENTERPRISE

STAR TREK

"...to explore strange new worlds..."

STAR DATE: _____

STAR TREK™

NCC-1701

U.S.S. ENTERPRISE

"LIVE LONG AND PROSPER." —SPOCK

STAR TREK

STAR DATE: _____

"These are the voyages of the Starship Enterprise."

TM ® & © 2006 Paramount Pictures. All rights reserved.

STAR TREK

"WARP SPEED AHEAD." —KIRK

NCC-1701

U.S.S. ENTERPRISE

STAR TREK

STAR DATE: _____

"...to seek out new life and new civilizations..."

U.S.S. ENTERPRISE
NCC-1701

TM ® & © 2006 Paramount Pictures. All rights reserved.

"IT'S A HUMAN CHARACTERISTIC TO LOVE LITTLE ANIMALS."

STAR TREK

NCC-1701

U.S.S. ENTERPRISE

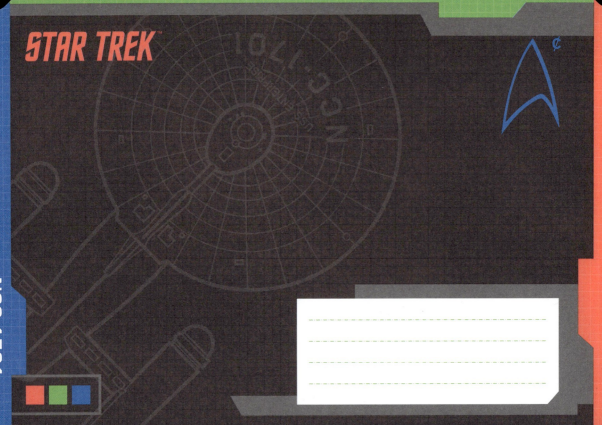

STAR TREK

"Space, the final frontier."

STAR DATE: _____

TM ® & © 2006 Paramount Pictures. All rights reserved.

STAR TREK

NCC-1701

U.S.S. ENTERPRISE

"I'VE ALREADY GOT A FEMALE TO WORRY ABOUT. HER NAME IS ENTERPRISE." – KIRK

STAR TREK

STAR DATE: _____

"...to boldly go where no man has gone before."

STAR TREK

NCC-1701

U.S.S. ENTERPRISE

"CRAZY WAY TO TRAVEL . . . SPREADING A MAN'S MOLECULES ALL OVER THE UNIVERSE." — MCCOY

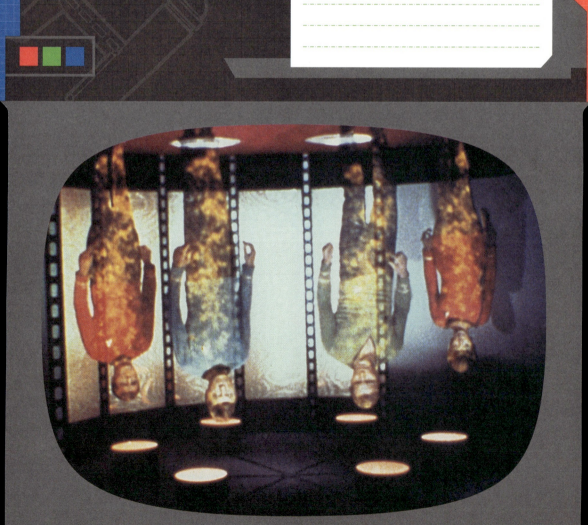

STAR DATE: _____

STAR TREK
"...to explore strange new worlds..."

TM ® & © 2006 Paramount Pictures. All rights reserved.

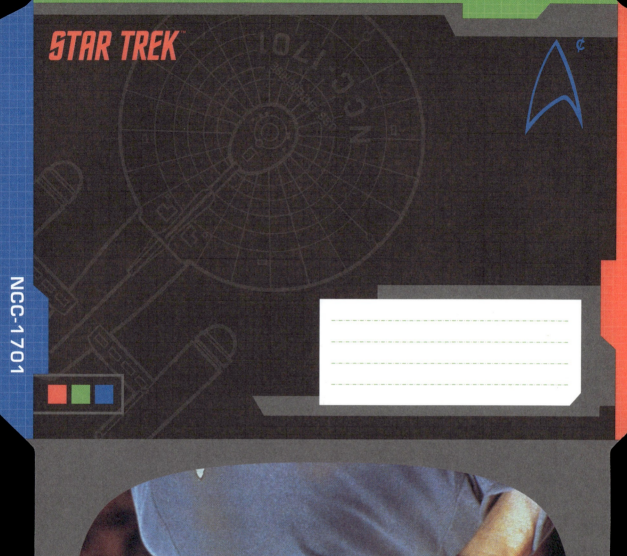
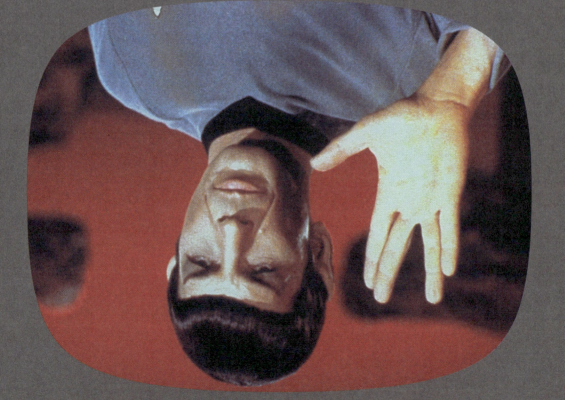

STAR TREK

"These are the voyages of the Starship Enterprise."

STAR DATE: _____

STAR TREK

"WARP SPEED AHEAD." —KIRK

NCC-1701

U.S.S. ENTERPRISE

STAR TREK

STAR DATE: _____

"...to seek out new life and new civilizations..."

U.S.S. ENTERPRISE
NCC-1701

STAR TREK

NCC-1701

U.S.S. ENTERPRISE

"IT'S A HUMAN CHARACTERISTIC TO LOVE LITTLE ANIMALS."

STAR DATE: _____

"Space, the final frontier."

TM ® & © 2006 Paramount Pictures. All rights reserved.

STAR TREK™

"I'VE ALREADY GOT A FEMALE TO WORRY ABOUT."

NCC-1701

U.S.S. ENTERPRISE

STAR DATE: _____

STAR TREK

"…to boldly go where no man has gone before."

TM ® & © 2006 Paramount Pictures. All rights reserved.

STAR TREK™

"CRAZY WAY TO TRAVEL... SPREADING A MAN'S

NCC-1701

U.S.S. ENTERPRISE

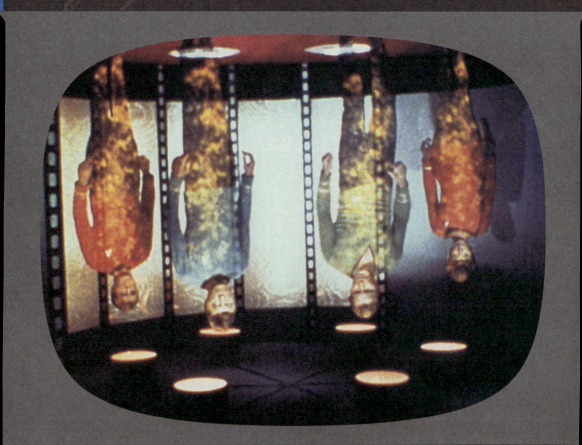

STAR TREK

"...to explore strange new worlds..."

STAR DATE: _____

TM ® & © 2006 Paramount Pictures. All rights reserved.

STAR TREK™

NCC-1701

U.S.S. ENTERPRISE

"LIVE LONG AND PROSPER." —SPOCK

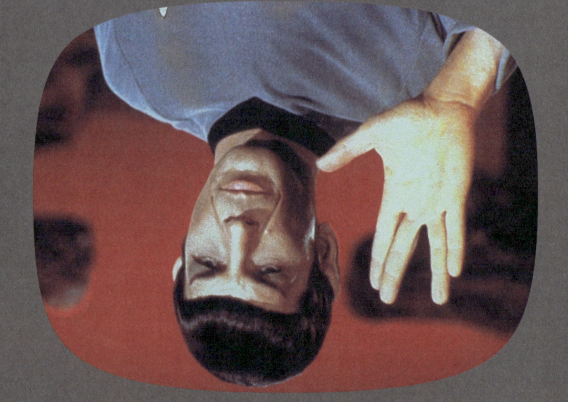

STAR TREK

STAR DATE: _____

"These are the voyages of the Starship Enterprise."

TM ® & © 2006 Paramount Pictures. All rights reserved.

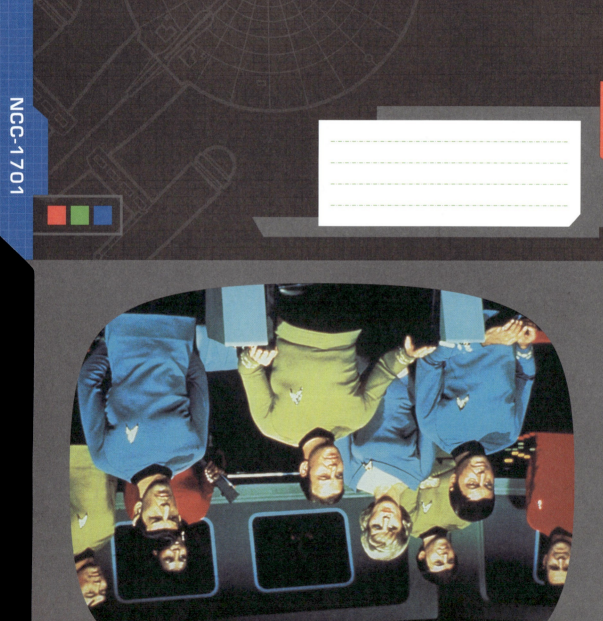

STAR TREK™

"WARP SPEED AHEAD." —KIRK

NCC-1701

U.S.S. ENTERPRISE

STAR DATE: _____

STAR TREK

"...to seek out new life and new civilizations..."

U.S.S. ENTERPRISE
NCC-1701

TM ® & © 2006 Paramount Pictures. All rights reserved.

"IT'S A HUMAN CHARACTERISTIC TO LOVE LITTLE ANIMALS,"

STAR TREK

NCC-1701

U.S.S. ENTERPRISE

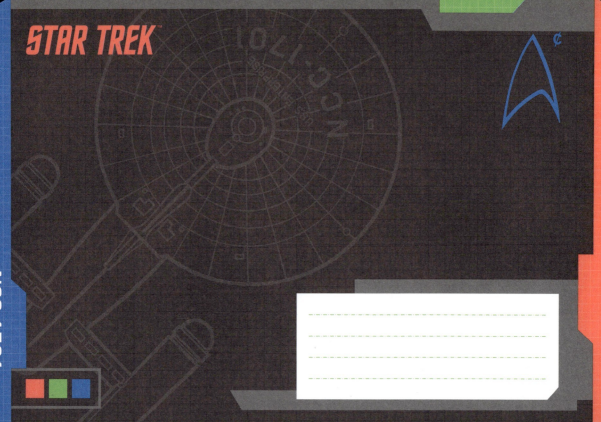

STAR TREK

"Space, the final frontier."

STAR DATE: _____

STAR TREK™

"I'VE ALREADY GOT A FEMALE TO WORRY ABOUT."

NCC-1701

U.S.S. ENTERPRISE

STAR TREK

STAR DATE: _____

"...to boldly go where no man has gone before."

STAR TREK™

"CRAZY WAY TO TRAVEL . . . SPREADING A MAN'S

NCC-1701

U.S.S. ENTERPRISE

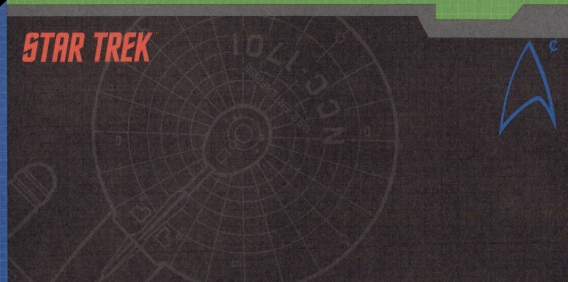

STAR TREK

"...to explore strange new worlds..."

STAR DATE: _____

STAR TREK™

NCC-1701

U.S.S. ENTERPRISE

"LIVE LONG AND PROSPER." —SPOCK

STAR TREK

STAR DATE: _____

"These are the voyages of the Starship Enterprise."

TM ® & © 2006 Paramount Pictures. All rights reserved.

STAR TREK

"WARP SPEED AHEAD." —KIRK

NCC-1701

U.S.S. ENTERPRISE

STAR TREK

STAR DATE: _____

"...to seek out new life and new civilizations..."

U.S.S. ENTERPRISE NCC-1701

TM ® & © 2006 Paramount Pictures. All rights reserved.

STAR TREK

"IT'S A HUMAN CHARACTERISTIC TO LOVE LITTLE ANIMALS,"

NCC-1701

U.S.S. ENTERPRISE